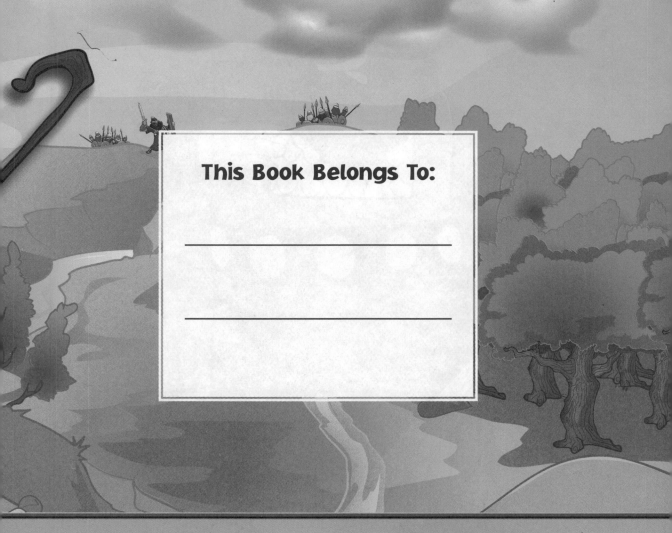

This Book Belongs To:

_____

_____

David and Goliath

There was a time when the Philistines were planning an attack against Israel. King Saul gathered his forces together to defend Israel. They were soon challenged by a fierce warrior of the Philistines, a giant nearly ten feet tall, named Goliath.

Goliath told the armies of Israel that he would be willing to fight any man from their army. If that man won, then all of the Philistines would be servants in the land of Israel. But if Goliath won, then Israel would have to serve Philistine.

But not one of the Israelite soldiers were brave enough to stand up against him, for no man had ever defeated him.

David was the youngest son in his family. His three older brothers had joined the King's army to fight against the Philistines. But David was too young, and so he stayed behind to watch his father's sheep.

One day David was told to take food to his brothers. When he reached them, he saw that the men of Israel were afraid of the fierce Goliath.

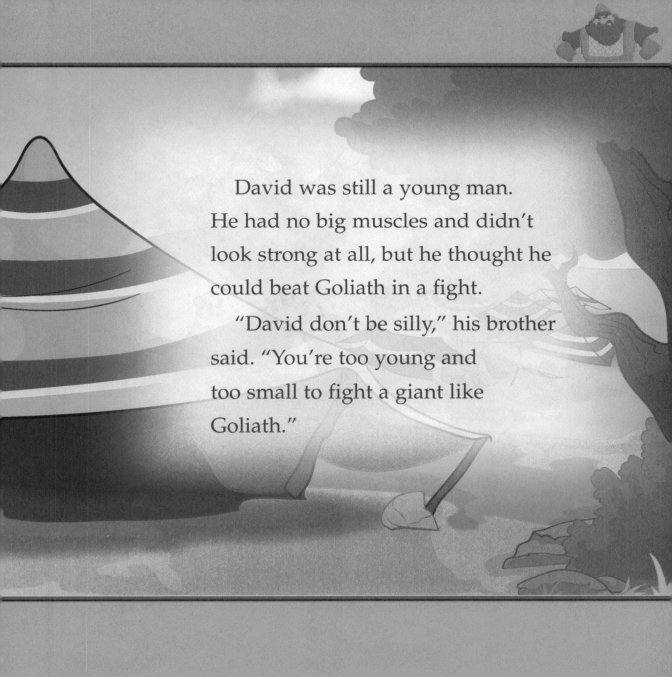

David was still a young man.
He had no big muscles and didn't
look strong at all, but he thought he
could beat Goliath in a fight.

"David don't be silly," his brother
said. "You're too young and
too small to fight a giant like
Goliath."

David went to King Saul and told him he was not afraid. The King said David was too young to fight Goliath, because he had never been in the army, and he'd never fought anyone.

David told King Saul that while watching his father's sheep, he had killed both lions and bears.

God had helped him then and
God would protect him against
Goliath.

King Saul was impressed with
David's bravery and agreed to let
the boy accept Goliath's challenge.
The King offered David armour and
a sword. But David refused, again
telling him that God would keep
him safe from harm.

With only a slingshot and a bag
of stones, David called out to the
mean-looking giant. "Goliath,
I have come from the armies
of Israel to challenge you."

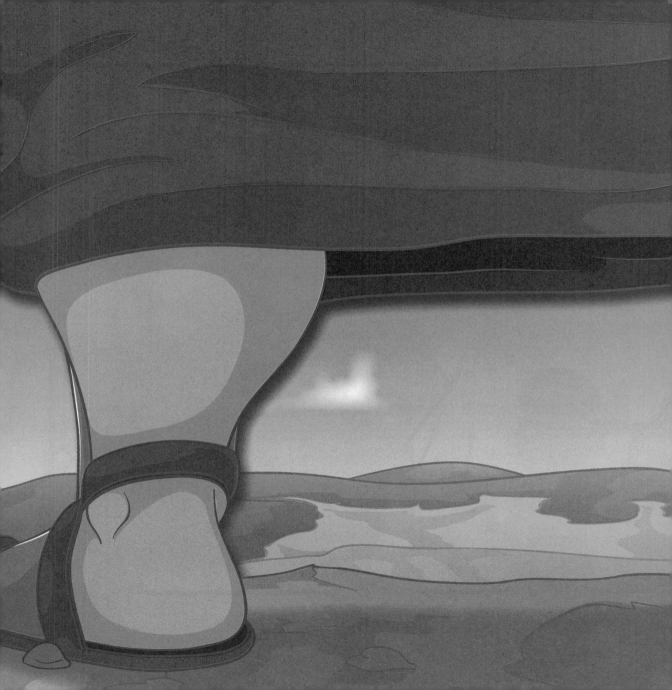

The giant Goliath stepped out before the army of Israel wearing a helmet of bronze and carrying a huge sword and shield. When he saw David, he began to laugh at the small boy his enemies had chosen to save them. "Is this a joke?" he called to them.

David answered Goliath. "You might be a giant with a giant's sword and shield, but I have God to protect me."

Goliath started toward David with his sword held high and a big smile on his face. He was certain he would strike David through the heart and take all of Israel as slaves for Philistine.

David was not afraid. He took one of the stones out of his bag and shot it with his slingshot. The stone hit Goliath right between the eyes and killed him instantly.